*There is a sticker at the front of my Bible that
I put there years ago. It says:
"This is the part where you find out who you are."*

*If God could whisper something in your heart as we
begin this time together it is just that.
You are about to unlock how to unearth the beauty of
scripture. As you find out who God is, you in turn find
out who you are.*

*My hope is that as you go through these pages you will
begin to find ways to understand scripture like never
before!*

XOXO

Introduction

If you've known me for any period of time, you've heard me say how much I love my Bible. Some might say I have a strange connection with it. Not only do I read my Bible daily, if I'm having a bad day, I will go home and I lay my Bible on my chest. Just it being there brings sheer calm over me.

But I wasn't always this way. When I first got saved, I didn't know the difference between Genesis and Revelation. Then I married into a house of theologians. Bryan's dad has a doctorate in theology. He is extremely intelligent. Bryan's uncle, John Hollar, was the dean of Christ For the Nations Institute for years. He's literally a walking concordance. You can ask Uncle John any scripture, and he'll spout it off to you.

They would sit at the dinner table talking about theology and debating all these different scriptural things. They would hear a sermon, then over lunch, they would give feedback on whether or not it was Hermeneutically correct. I was like some of you are right now. I didn't know what theology was and could barely pronounce Hermeneutics nevertheless understand it. I didn't even know what Genesis 1 said. I knew nothing. But hearing them talk about the Scripture with such reverence and passion put a desire inside of me: I didn't understand it, but there was something in me that wanted what they had.

Every time the Word of God is brought forth, we have a choice to make. It's the same choice those in Biblical times made when Jesus spoke the Word: Either they chose to believe what He said or to walk away.

Some people when they deem someone more spiritually mature—often because of insecurities and feelings of inadequacy—they push away and they reject what's truth. But for others, hearing the Word of God calls them to a pursuit. That's what it did for me. I didn't know what they had but I knew I wanted it. Psalm 42:7 talks about a deep calling out to deep. That is what happened when I heard the Word spoken around me. The Word called me deeper. And that is my prayer for you as you read through this book, that deep will call unto deep. That your spirit will go on a deep pursuit of the Word of God and you will come to love your Bible like never before.

My goal is that you gain an appreciation and love for the Word in a whole new way.

So can I pray over you and our time together before we move on?

Jesus, thank you for making Your Word come alive. Lord let our hearts be good ground for the Word to fall. Right now we weed out any preconceived notion that we're not holy enough, that we're not good enough to come to You, that we've messed up too much, that You don't love us. Lord, we approach You with new fresh faith. Show us who You are. Give us this day our daily bread. Lord, we're seeking a fresh word from You. In Jesus' name.
Amen.

Now let's dig into the Word.

Chapter 1

LOVING YOUR BIBLE

*The Word is like a woman.
She'll undress for the one who loves her.*
- John Hollar

    I love to read. I read books of inspiring true stories and beautiful love stories and biographies of incredible people who have accomplished amazing things. I know a lot of people who love to read like I do, but they don't love to read their Bible. What they don't realize is that the Bible isn't meant to be read like any other book. It isn't a novel to be read straight through. It isn't just inspiring stories. The Bible is living, active, and sharper than a two-edged sword. Everything you will ever need can be found in the Bible.
    Some Christians pick up their Bible and they only see the surface. They have read and know the famous Bible stories, but their reading ends there.
    Maybe you've even done this yourself. Perhaps you've started with great intentions to read your Bible every day. Or you've started a one-year Bible plan. But eventually, you read a book or chapter that isn't so interesting. Parts of it are hard to get through—let's just say it, it's boring. It's okay. That's not blasphemy. Maybe you don't think you understand what some of it—

or a lot of it—is saying. So eventually, you stop reading. We've all done it.

Think about the quote at the beginning of this chapter. "The Word is like a woman. She'll undress for the one who loves her." Isn't that beautiful imagery? Whenever we approach the Word in an intimate, loving way, there is depth in it.

I see clothed people everyday. But my husband, Bryan, knows me in a deeper way. And that is the kind of deep, intimate relationship we should have with our Bible.

Throughout the Bible, the Greek word *ginosko* is translated to English as "to know," which is the same word God used about Adam knowing Eve. It speaks of a deep intimacy. This is the kind of knowing God wants for us with His Word. Paul reinforces this in Ephesians 1:17, saying that his hope was for the Ephesian church to come into a deep and intimate relationship with Jesus.

The result of that relationship with Jesus is expressed in verse 18, "By having the eyes of your heart flooded with light, so that you can know and understand the hope to which He has called you, and how rich is His glorious inheritance in the saints (His set-apart ones)."

Let me unpack this verse.

"The eyes of their heart would be flooded with light."
Hearts don't have eyes so this almost seems silly , but what Paul was saying is that we all see things through the lens of our hearts. A lot of us have experienced past pain. That pain changes how we see the world around us. As we come to know God in deep intimate ways, He floods the darkest areas of our hearts with His light.

"Know and understand the hope to which He has called you." Through knowing God in a deep and intimate way, I am able to understand my calling in Him. Notice that Paul wrote the, "hope of our calling." You may not be sure what you are called by God to do, but I can encourage you that whatever God has called you to will be something good.

The way you discover your calling is through knowing Him

in deeper ways.

"Inheritance in the saints." God has a reward for all who seek Him. When we find Him, we also find all that our hearts have ever searched for. It is there that we find fulfillment. The inheritance that Paul wrote about here is not material possessions but about making a difference. Deep inside every heart there is a yearning to have a life that matters. The more we know God the more our life makes a difference, not just today but in eternity.

A lot of people read the Word and only see surface. They see the Bible stories and the familiar scriptures. But they don't have that kindred kind of love for their Bible. I hear people say all the time, "I hate reading my Bible." Well, she's like a woman. She'll undress for the one who loves her. The more deeply you fall in love with your Bible, the more deeply it will fall in love with you.

Before this can happen, we need to break off the myths that have held you back from reading and loving your Bible.

What Lie Have You Believed?

We have access to something that no other generation had access to. Before Jesus came, the only people who read the Torah—the first five books of the Bible—were men. Women could not even be in a room where the Word of God was being taught until Jesus came. If you think about it, Jesus started the first women's liberation movement. When the Bible shows women following Jesus, it was because, for the first time, a Messianic teacher welcomed them into the room to hear the Word of God.

There are people in China today giving their lives for the Bible. There are people being beheaded in Turkey for the book that we have in our homes but leave unopened to collect dust because we have bought into a lie.

We aren't the only ones who have believed this lie. The devil hasn't changed his tactics. All the way back to the beginning in

Genesis 3:1, it says, "Now the serpent was more crafty (subtle, skilled in deceit) than any living creature of the field which the Lord God had made. And the serpent (Satan) said to the woman, "Can it really be that God has said, 'You shall not eat from any tree of the garden'?" The devil prompted Eve to question what God said.

Now Eve had walked in perfect communion with God in the Garden of Eden. There was no sin. There were no distractions. There were no phones, no Facebook, or kid's soccer practices to keep her from spending time with God. In fact, the Bible says, in the cool of the day, God came down and walked with her in the garden. If anybody knew what God had said, wouldn't it be Eve? She spent time with Him. She strolled with Him. She talked with Him. But when the enemy came, he made her question what God's Word said and what God had told her. And we know what happened, right? When she questioned God's Word, she ate from the tree of knowledge of good and evil. She did the one thing God had warned her not to do.

My husband, Bryan, always jokes that because of Eve, women can never decide what to eat. Right? Maybe that was part of the curse. I mean, it didn't turn out well for our girl, Eve, so it feels like the whole world is lying on our shoulders if we choose the wrong thing. In all seriousness, though, the enemy got her to question God's Word, and his goal is to do the same with you and me. Even Jesus was tempted by the devil in Luke 4. How did the devil come at Jesus? He questioned the Word of God. Over and over, the devil asked Jesus, "Doesn't the Word say...?" But Jesus responded with the truth of the Word.

The enemy is going to attack you. That's a guarantee. He knows the Word, but he wants to see if you know the Word. Because the Word is what will set you free; not knowing the Word will keep you in bondage. Hosea 4:6 tells us, "My people perish for a lack of knowledge." In other words, what you don't know is hurting you. We think we're going to be set free by what we already know, so we busy ourselves with so many things in the natural that we forget the most important thing is lying on our coffee table or our nightstand right in front of us.

So what have you believed that has kept you from your Bible? I'm going to bust these lies wide open. And as you read on, I want you to break-up with whatever lie the enemy has whispered into your ear to keep you from the very Word of God that can set you free.

Lie #1 "I don't understand the Bible."
This is the same lie Eve believed. It is the biggest lie that the enemy will tell us about the Word of God. "I don't understand what God is saying." This lie messed Eve up royally, and it will mess us up too. People tell me, "I wish I could read and understand my Bible like you do." I am here to tell you that you can.

Let me prove it to you: Do you speak English? Yes. Can you read English? Yes. Is your Bible written in English? Yes. Can you read any other book in English and understand it? Yes. So it's a lie that you can't understand the Bible.

Lie #2. "I don't have time to read the Bible."
Have you checked your social media in the last 24 hours? Have you eaten? You've had time to call your girlfriend. You've had time to brush your teeth. You've even had time to pick up this book. I'm not trying to be judgey. I do all of those things too... but only after my time in the Word.

So many Christians make time for the natural things, but so often, we neglect our spirit. This is why so many Christians are frustrated. We feel like God's not giving us "all these things" like we have seen promised in the Word. The job is not working out. The marriage is flailing. The kids are a mess. But it's because they aren't seeking the Kingdom first. They're busy seeking "all these things" without doing their part. In other words, they're saying, "God, I want You to do what I want You to do, but I won't do what You tell me to do."

Imagine if I told my kids that if they did one thing, they would get everything they wanted. They would get the iPad; they would get the Xbox; they would get to go to Disney all they want; they get to do all the things; but I needed them to do one thing first. Do you think they would be willing to do that one thing?

Now what if my kids didn't do the one thing I asked them to do, and they came to me and were frustrated because they didn't get the iPad or the trip to Disney or all the other stuff? My answer would be, "I'm so sorry. But I didn't have an unfair expectation. I only asked you to do one thing."

Isn't that what most Christians are doing? We want everything that God has, but we don't want to give Him anything that we have.

How strong would your marriage be if you never spent time together? What if you went home and you told your spouse, "Babe, I love you, but from now on I'm going to see you once a week on Sundays. I'll come visit you for an hour, and I'll talk to you when I'm there. But for the rest of the week, babe, we're going to do our own thing." Would your spouse be down for that? Because I know Bryan wouldn't. It wouldn't go well, right? You wouldn't get all these things. There would be some lonely, cold nights.

Yet that's the way we approach God. God, give me what I want, but I don't really want to spend time with you. How would that make you feel if your kids were like, "Hey, I don't have time to come see you. So can you just direct deposit some money to my account." As a parent, I can't even imagine. But that's how we treat God when we say we don't have time for Him and His Word, but we have time for our friends, our phones, our social media, and our Netflix shows. God wants to do so much in us and for us. All we have to do is put down the phone or the remote and pick up our Bible.

Lie #3. "The Bible is only for pastors or for teachers."

This makes me so sad and yet I hear it all the time. People tell me, "You're a pastor. Of course you read your Bible." Let's get this straight real quick. I read my Bible every day before I was a pastor. I read my Bible every day when I was working like a dog at Sonic, taking corny dogs out to cars and going home smelling like grease. I was in the Word every single day back then.

I don't read my Bible because I'm a pastor. I read my Bible because I'm a Christian. Because I'm a daughter of the King.

People have said to me, "I want to understand my Bible better so I'm going to go to seminary."

So I ask them, "How much time do you spend in your Bible now?"

"Oh I don't read it."

Wait, what? Getting a degree isn't going to make you get into a personal habit of reading the Bible. That would be like saying, "I'm going to go to school to be a fitness trainer so I can lose weight." It doesn't make sense.

You do not need to go to seminary to read and understand the Bible. We think, "If I was a pastor or a teacher, I'd be able to understand." John 1:1–4 says, "In the beginning was the Word, and the Word was with God, and the Word was God. He was in the beginning with God. All things were made through Him, and without Him nothing was made that was made. In Him was life, and the life was the light of men." This is all pointing back to the Word. The Word was available to all men, that means all humankind. It doesn't say to those with the profession of ministry. Or to those who are super-Christians and really, really holy. No, the Word was for all men. It was for everyone. The Word of God is for YOU.

If I was the enemy and I knew that your faith would overcome the world, and I also knew that your faith would come by hearing and hearing by the Word, then the number one thing I would keep you from is the Word of God. The devil knows how powerful your faith can be, and his objective is to do whatever it takes to convince you to stay out of the Word in any way that he can.

Don't give the devil any space to lie to you in this area any more. Instead, choose to make the Word of God a priority. The Bible is the key that gives you access to everything in God. And that journey begins here: by learning how to love your Bible and understand the scriptures more and more.

Chapter 2

KNOWING YOUR BIBLE

Early in my faith journey, I wanted to learn and memorize as much scripture as I could. Like I mentioned in the introduction, Bryan's Uncle John is a walking concordance. You can ask him any scripture, and he'll spout it off. I told Uncle John, "I want to know and love my Bible like you love yours." So I asked him to teach me.

What God starts with us should never end with us, so I am passing down to you what he taught me.

The first step to loving your Bible is to find one translation that you love and stay with that translation for the rest of your life. That's a pretty heavy commitment, right? Until death do us part. You might have to test out a few translations, but find one you love.

My favorite is Joyce Meyer's *Amplified Bible*. I will be 95 years old still reading my Joyce Meyer's *Amplified*. I joke around saying that *The Amplified* is the Bible Jesus reads just because I love it, but one translation is not necessarily any better than the others. My husband, Bryan, reads *New King James Version*. If you ask Uncle John, he says the best direct translation of the original text is either *New King James* or *King James*, then *The Amplified Bible*. From there, it's really just a matter of preference.

Be careful that you choose a translation and not a paraphrase. There is nothing wrong with reading a paraphrase. In fact, it can really open your eyes to a scripture in a new way. However, a paraphrase is not a direct translation of the original written text. Often, the author of a paraphrase will interpret the text instead of directly translating it. *The Message Bible* is one example. Reading scripture from it as a reference can be eye-opening, but you have to remember that it is not always accurate to the original text.

If you want to compare translations versus paraphrases/interpretations look at John 5:1–8 across different versions and note how some versions have whole verses excluded from them. This can help you determine which version to read and study.

There isn't anything wrong with mixing it up sometimes. Right now, *The Passion Translation* is speaking to my soul in a deep way. But I don't have the same spiritual connection with my *Passion Translation*, so after reading it for a while, my spirit begins to crave my *Amplified Bible* again.

I have come to not only read in the same translation but buy my Bibles from the same maker. Here's why. We are visual creatures. When you memorize a scripture, you will first memorize how it lands on the page more than the scripture itself. So if I'm holding my Joyce Meyer's *Amplified Bible*, I might not be able to tell you that the scripture reference is Roman 10:9, but I know the feel of the page, how far it is into the Bible, and my mind can picture the way the verse looks on the page. So I can take you straight to it, even though I don't know it chapter and verse.

There are so many ways to access Bible translations now through the Internet or Bible apps. However, I highly recommend reading from a physical Bible. I'm not against reading on your phone. My pastor loves to read on his phone. But our phones are great distractions. If I read my Bible on my phone, before I know it, text messages are coming through, people are calling, Facebook notifications are showing up. I am distracted too easily on my phone. When I spend time with God, I want to give Him

100% of my attention and not be distracted by everything else.

Another reason I love a paper Bible is because I enjoy Bible journaling. Pastor Lawrence Neisent teaches a method that I like to follow. Each day in my Bible reading, I journal a note of what is happening in my life on the page that I am reading. I have done this for years.

When I was pregnant and had a miscarriage, I journaled in my Bible through that time. I journaled to the child I would have next after the miscarriage, who turned out to be my daughter, Brailey. There were dark days and then bright days. Then when my son, Bear, was in the NICU and we didn't know if he was going to make it, I journaled in my Bible through those dark days and the bright days.

One day when my children read it, it will probably be like reading the Psalms. But it is a sweet and precious treasure to have Bibles on my shelf that are threadbare and worn out, but in them, I can take you to the scripture that I read the day that Brailey received Jesus into her heart. I can show you the scripture I read as God healed Bear's back. You don't get that in a digital Bible. A digital Bible is not going to leave a heritage to your children. So I would encourage you to get a paper Bible if you don't have one.

Even more practically, at the end of each book of the Bible, I write the month and year that I finished reading it. This process helps me keep up with what I have and haven't read.

These are my processes, and maybe yours will be different. But I encourage you to have a paper Bible in a translation that you enjoy. Remove as many obstacles and distractions as you can so that you can focus to read the Word of God.

Chapter 3
DOCTRINE VS. THEOLOGY

Every year, our church does a series called "You Asked For It" where Bryan and I answer hard questions that the members of our church have submitted. Do you know what the number one question in this series is every year? How do I grow my faith? But Romans 10:17 tells us the answer. "So faith *comes* from hearing [what is told], and what is heard comes by the [preaching of the] message concerning Christ."

The problem is we want the results without the work. We want to lose weight without working out and without eating right. We want all the blessings of God without spending time in the Word. We want a cheaper process. God doesn't care about all that. Romans 10:14 says, "But how will people call on Him in whom they have not believed? And how will they believe in Him of whom they have not heard? And how will they hear without a preacher (messenger)?"

Theology Explained

You will believe whatever theology you put yourself under. Now, most people would use the term doctrine for what is actually theology. What's the difference? Theology can change. Doctrine remains the same. Theology is our thought process about the scripture. Doctrine is scripturally proven.

For a lot of people, their theology is ever changing. Your theology about the Holy Spirit might change based on what church you are attending. Your theology about prosperity might change depending on the message you are hearing. But the doctrine of the Holy Spirit and prosperity never changes.

Some churches might tell you a doctrine that's different than your theology. That doesn't make them wrong or you right. I'll show you later in this chapter how you can determine if something is correct doctrine or not. If you can show me in the scripture where you stand—we'll talk about that here in just a second—then you'll be able to stand on your own two feet.

A lot of us think that if Jesus showed up in the flesh today that we would begin to align our beliefs with what He said, but that's not necessarily true. Think about in the New Testament when God was doing so many things among the people, but the Sanhedrein, who were the religious leaders of the day, were upset. Then John 6:66 says "many of His disciples abandoned Him, and no longer walked with Him." They turned away from the truth of the gospel of Jesus, because they were under a teaching that found the truth to be wrong. So whatever theology you place yourself under will become the foundation to which your belief system is formed.

That's why there are churches gathered together under the belief that there is no such thing as prosperity, that the Holy Spirit isn't good for today, and that acts of miracles and healing have passed away. Guess what? Everybody under that belief system is broke, sick, and lacking in miracles. They would say their beliefs are proven in their body of believers. I would argue that the thought process being taught has developed the way they believe, because faith comes by hearing and hearing by the Word.

Jesus even said, "Pay attention to what you hear. By your own standard of measurement [that is, to the extent that you study spiritual truth and apply godly wisdom] it will be measured to you [and you will be given even greater ability to respond]—and more will be given to you besides" (Mark 4:24 AMP).

The teaching you expose yourself to justifies your beliefs which in turn gets you exactly what you believed and when you believe, you speak (see 2 Corinthians 4:13). You are the biggest prophet over your own life and what you speak you are calling into existence.

Personally, I don't position myself under certain people. When they start preaching brokenness and poverty, I won't sit under it. I don't want that kind of hearing to come in to my heart, because I'll eventually believe what I'm hearing and those things will start happening to me.

Let me prove this to you in Acts 8:5–6, "Philip [the deacon, not the apostle] went down to the city of Samaria and proclaimed the Christ (the Messiah) to them [the people]; And great crowds of people with one accord listened to and heeded what was said by Philip." What did they do? Listened and heeded. If you write in your Bible, underline that phrase.

Notice what Philip did in verse 5. He "proclaimed Christ." In other words, he preached Jesus. It goes on to say, "as they heard him and watched the miracles and wonders which he kept performing [from time to time]. For foul spirits came out of many who were possessed by them, screaming and shouting with a loud voice, and many who were suffering from palsy or were crippled were restored to health. And there was great rejoicing in that city."

Jesus told them time and time again, not only to be hearers of the Word but doers also. There was a response in their heart to what the Word was saying. As they heard Philip preach the Word—faith comes by hearing and hearing by the Word—they also saw miracles and wonders happening. They were hearing and they were seeing at the same time.

You are going to get to a point in your Christian walk where when you hear something and your faith is big enough for it, then you're going to see things instantaneously change in your surroundings. When we begin to position ourselves where we're hearing the unadulterated message of Jesus, we will see it working at the same time. It's not going to be waiting and believing and believing and believing. It's hearing and seeing.

The Sanhedrin were religious, and they were preaching their theology. In other words, they were not preaching Christ. They didn't believe Jesus was the Son of God. The people under the theology of the Sanhedrin grew bitter and angry, and they were the ones who captured and crucified Jesus. They were the ones who hunted down and crucified the disciples.

The theology you put yourself under is going to create the results you see in your life. If you don't like the results you're getting, check your thinking. Check who and what you're listening to. But the people who listened to Christ and Him being preached, they saw miracles. They heard and they saw.

In our lives, the Bible is the most important thing because it is the Word of God. In John 1:1, it says, "And the Word became flesh." When you say you don't like you're Bible, you're saying, "I don't like Jesus." When you say you don't believe that part of the Bible, you're saying, "I don't believe Jesus." The people in Acts saw miracles like the lame walking, sick being healed, people demonically oppressed getting set free, because they heard the Word of God preached and they acted on it. With the Word and the anointing of the Holy Spirit, when you say "In Jesus' name," there is no difference between you and Jesus Himself.

If I was the devil, I would get inside your head so much that you're afraid to read the Word, believe the Word, or to speak the Word.

Most Christians don't know a single scripture. I'm not saying this judgmentally. I'm saying this because if we want things to change, we have to get in the Bible.

What Is Doctrine?

We call everything doctrine, but doctrine is actually what is scripturally sound.

For example, look at Job. Job lost everything, so could we take Job and make it doctrine because it's in scripture and all scripture is God-breathed and God-inspired? What about "Jesus wept" (John 11:35)? If we consider everything doctrine then we could read that scripture and say that we should be weeping all the time because Jesus wept. But that's not how it works.

How do you determine if something in scripture is doctrine or not?
   1. Is it referenced in the Old Testament?
   2. Did Jesus teach it?
   3. Did the apostles teach it?
   4. Did the New Testament church practice it?

If those four things cannot be found, it cannot be doctrine. It doesn't matter what your grandma said. It doesn't matter what your old church said. If it doesn't like up with scripture in these four ways, then it isn't Biblical doctrine.

One of the biggest topics that people argue doctrine over is the Holy Spirit. They don't believe the Holy Spirit is for today, or they don't believe in the gifts of the Holy Spirit. I tell them to show me scripturally where the Old Testament talked against it, where Jesus spoke against it, where the apostles didn't practice it, and where the New Testament church didn't do it. If you can't show me that, then it is simply your theology, but don't call it doctrine. That is your thought process about Holy Spirit.

Let's use this example and find out what scriptural doctrine says about the Holy Spirit based on these four qualifications.

1. Is it referenced in the Old Testament? Joel 2:28 says, "I will pour out My Spirit upon all flesh; and your sons and daughters shall prophecy, your old men shall dream dreams, your young men shall see vision."

2. Did Jesus preach it? Jesus said, "These signs will accompany those who believed: In My name they will cast out demons, they will speak in new tongues; they will pick up serpents, and if they drink anything deadly, it will not hurt them; they will lay hands on the sick, and they will get well" (Mark 16:17–18). He's talking about the baptism of the Holy Spirit. Then He also said in John 14:12, "Anyone who believes in Me [as Savior] will do these things that I do; and he will do even greater works than these."

3. Do the apostles teach it? When the apostle Paul came to the Ephesian church, he asked them if they had received the Holy Spirit (Acts 19:1–6).

4. Did the New Testament church practice it? We see the New Testament church practicing it as they were all filled with the Holy Spirit on the day of Pentecost in Acts 2.

Our conclusion is: yes, we can say that being filled with the Holy Spirit is doctrine.

Another example commonly debated is God wanting us to be financially prosperous.

1. Is it referenced in the Old Testament? In Genesis 2:11–12, "The first [river] is named Pishon; it flows around the entire land of Havilah, where there is gold. The gold of that land is good; bdellium (a fragrant, valuable resin) and the onyx stone are found there." The land God placed Adam in to live was filled with gold, pearl, and onyx. Adam didn't need gold, pearl, or onyx. There wasn't even an economic system at the time when Adam was formed. But God put Adam in a place of abundance, knowing what he would need beforehand and making sure he was surrounded by it. And that's only the beginning of the Bible. There are so many more examples throughout the Old Testament of God's people being exceedingly wealthy.

2. Did Jesus preach it? Not one time did Jesus ever speak against wealth. In fact, He told us that whenever we sow, we would reap one hundred, sixty, or thirty fold. In other words, Jesus' plan for your life is for you to reap one hundred fold, which is more than enough.

3. Do the apostles teach it? The apostles were exceedingly wealthy. They were abundantly blessed always having everything they needed.

4. Did the New Testament church practice it? In Acts 3, the New Testament church was blessed in everything they did.

When we see these four things happening, we can say that God's will for our life is for us to be blessed because we have those four Biblical legs to stand on.

Understanding these principles will help you in your lifelong growth with God.

Chapter 4
FAST-FOOD VS. GOURMET DEVOTIONS

Do you remember every meal you ate this week? I'm assuming the answer is no. You might even have to take a minute to remember what you had for breakfast yesterday.

But are you living and breathing right now? Are you healthy? The reason you are living, breathing, and healthy right now is because you ate. Even though every meal wasn't memorable, it sustained you and got you where you are today.

When the Israelites were living in the wilderness, manna fell on the earth every morning, and it only stayed good for a day before it would spoil. So they would gather just enough for that day. The Word of God is our spiritual manna. Every day we need this manna to live. Every day we need a daily dose of the Word of God to stay spiritually healthy.

How many mind-blowing meals did you have in the last month? I had a really good steak a few weeks ago, but that is certainly not my daily diet. Even though every meal isn't memorable, every meal sustains us.

There are times when I read my Bible and it is a deep, holy moment where I feel the heavens open up and the angels descending. In those times, I journal all that God is speaking to me. I take notes on the new, deep revelations He is showing me.

But I'll be honest, some days I read my Bible and I don't even remember what I just read. Most of the time, it is simply reading the scripture and thanking God for it. "In the beginning was the Word and the Word was with God." That's good, Lord, thank You. "Sing to the Lord a new song." That's good. I'm going to do that.

Take the box off your private devotions that they have to be an anointed hour long experience. Sometimes, they are. Sometimes, the presence of God will be so rich that you may not want to leave. But it's okay if every day isn't that way.

When you're on the run and you've got kid's practices, work, school, and lots of events, do you make a huge gourmet meal that night? No, you go through Chick-fil-A drive-thru. (This is not sponsored; I just really love Chick-fil-A!) I mean, McDonald's looks good when you're starving, right? Everybody says they don't eat at McDonald's, but for some reason, they sell a billion burgers. I'll admit it. I lose all standards for food when I am hungry and on-the-go.

Sometimes your personal devotion is going to be fast-food devotion time. Maybe you listen to the audio Bible or a podcast while you are in the shower. Most of the time, I read a scripture that speaks to me, then every single day while I'm in the shower, I listen to a podcast with a Word of God teaching. Joyce Meyer is my multivitamin. I listen to her every single morning. You can listen to the audio Bible on your way to work. You are getting ready and driving to work anyway, so add the Word of God to it.

That's a drive-thru, fast-food devotion. But if you ate McDonald's for every meal, you would be sick. Have you watched *Super Size Me*? It's not good. You have to have a balance. But if I ate it all the time, I'd be sick. The same is true for fast-food devotion time.

You should have those deep moments with the Lord too. But don't be hard on yourself because every day doesn't look like that. It doesn't have to be Instagrammable with a candle, cup of coffee, and your journal. That's preparing the big four-course gourmet meal. My devotion time looks like that maybe twice a week. So take the pressure off yourself.

Feed your spirit each day just as you feed your body. Remember every meal sustains you.

Chapter 5
UNDERSTANDING THE FOUR GOSPELS

Many people consider the four Gospels redundant because they are too similar or contradictory of each other because they aren't exactly the same. What they don't realize is that nothing is wasted or unintentional in God. What I'm going to show you will have you seeing the Gospels and the Bible differently, instead of just approaching them as is.

Why do we have four Gospels? Matthew, Mark, Luke, and John each reveal something different about Jesus. This was foretold in Ezekiel 1:10, "Regarding the form *and* appearance of their faces: they [each] had the face of a man [in front], and each had the face of a lion on the right side, and the face of an ox on the left side; all four also had the face of an eagle [at the back of their heads]." There are four faces on this: the man, the eagle, the lion, and the ox.

The man speaks of the humanity of Christ. The lion, which is the king of all the animals, represents victory and boldness in Jesus. The ox, the beast of burden, represents Christ's willingness to serve and carry our weights. The eagle shows the soaring, unrestrained power of God.

This relates to all four of the Gospels. Matthew is the man. Mark is the lion. Luke is the ox. John is the eagle.

If you need victory in your life, which Gospel do you want to read? Mark talks about the lion, the king of all kings. His perspective will be from the stance of victory.

Matthew reminds me of the humanity of Christ. Matthew begins his account with the genealogy of Christ proving that family tree he came from (Matthew 1:1–17). Jesus was 100% God but He was also 100% man. When reading Matthew's account of Jesus' life I am reminded that God is willing to go on the journey with me as I overcome shortcomings and failures. Matthew's Gospel account spends so much time giving practical instruction that Jesus told the disciples. This is where we find the famous sermon on the mount (Matthew 5–7) and the Lord's prayer (Matthew 6:9–13).

Luke is the ox, and the ox represents the servant and the bearing of our burdens. Time and time again Luke talks about Jesus taking our burdens. He repeatedly tells us not to worry. In this season I am in while I'm writing this, I have needed to hear that every day, so I have been reading through Luke then making a u-turn and reading through it again.

Three of the gospels take a perspective from the earth up. One has the perspective from heaven down. Remember, John is representative of the eagle. He gives a totally different perspective. Everything in John begins with a broad view, then he zooms in. He reaches all the way to the beginning and gives back story: "In the beginning was the Word" (John 1:1); "[Jesus] noticed a man blind from his birth" (9:1). John often tells the end of the story at the beginning as well. "Judas Iscariot, the one of [Jesus'] disciples who was about to betray Him" (12:4).

So each of the four Gospels give us a different perspective, even when they tell the same story.

Think about this in a real life scenario. I often go running with some of my friends. All of us have different backgrounds and are in different seasons of life. A while ago, we went on a summer run early in the morning before the sun had come up. Running through a residential area, we passed a particular house just as a guy was walking out the door. When I looked at him, he started taking off his shirt and hollered something at us.

Of course, I started running faster, thinking this guy was a pervert. When my friends caught up to me, I said, "Man, that was weird." They all agreed, and we finished our run and went about our day.

Back at the office, I couldn't let it go. A couple of the girls who were running with me were at the office too, and I said, "That was weird when that guy came out of the house, took his shirt off, and said, 'Woo, better get running girls. It's getting hot. It's summertime.'"

One of my friends laughed and said, "That's not what he said. He said, 'Wow, it's getting hot this summer."

Then another said, "No, that's not what he said. He said, 'Wow, I love summer.' And he wasn't taking his shirt off. He was putting it on because he was going to work."

By then we were laughing at how different our memories were, so we texted one of the other girls to find out what she thought. As soon as we brought it up, she said, "Oh my gosh, he's a pedophile."

Five people, five different backgrounds. We all had different stories. The girl who perceived this guy as a pedophile was sexually molested as a child. Her past pain changed the way she saw things.

In reading the four Gospels, we need to take into account that they were four men with four differing backgrounds and perspectives. This is why there are some stories that are exclusive to one Gospel. Each of their accounts of the gospel is important and shows us a different facet of Jesus' ministry.

I like to psychoanalyze the authors and get inside their head. It opens up a new perspective reading through the Bible to know their backgrounds and experiences. So let's look at each of the authors of the gospels.

The Gospel of Matthew

Matthew was a tax collector. His Gospel talks more about money than any other of the three. The message he heard Jesus preach was completely different than the other disciples because of his background and the place of his deepest hurt. We don't see things as they are. We see them as we are.

Before he became a tax collector, Matthew was studying to be a rabbi. To become a Jewish rabbi, young men had to memorize all five books of the Torah—which are the first five books of the Bible—before the age of twelve. (Can you imagine? How many Christians have ten scriptures memorized?) Then they would go through a selection process, and the elders would weed out the young men they thought were not cut out to be rabbi. Matthew was rejected.

Sometimes what we think is out biggest setback is really our biggest setup. Matthew would never have been one of the twelve disciples if he had been accepted as a rabbi. Instead, he was prepared for what God was about to do through the ministry of Jesus.

Remember earlier we learned that the Gospel of Matthew shows the humanity of Christ. Tax collectors were hated and dishonest, yet Jesus asked Matthew to be His disciple. Jesus' humanity stood out to him since he was found by God in what some would call the lowest position of their time.

How meaningful it must have been to Matthew when Jesus told him, "Don't worry. I'm not going to let you down. Other people may not have chosen you, but I've chosen you."

The Gospel of Mark

The author of the Gospel of Mark is unknown. Based on what I have read and studied, I agree with those who believe the author was Peter. Interestingly, in his retelling, Peter does not mention the story of him walking on water. Some say that he didn't put his name on the book because of the fear of his failure. So he chose to put Mark's instead. That makes it deep doesn't it? He wrote his account through the lens of his past failure. When having the opportunity, he didn't want to talk about how he failed. My heart breaks reading Mark 14:47 where Peter calls himself a bystander.

We know it was Peter in this verse because of John's account in John 18:10. Years had passed since Peter had done things that he was less than proud of, but the shame of his mistakes still lingered.

Mark is one of the shortest books, because Peter was awaiting execution. This might be why his focus turns to the suffering of Christ in chapter 8, as he too was sharing in Christ's suffering. Before he was executed, he made sure that his account was written. That's why some of the timeline is flawed in Mark; he was writing as fast as he could before being executed by religious leaders.

Peter describes Jesus as a servant fourteen times in his Gospel account. He spends a lot of time focusing on religious leaders.

The Gospel of Luke

Luke was a doctor, so there are more medical diagnoses in the book of Luke than anywhere else. He was not a disciple of Jesus. In fact, he was saved after Jesus' resurrection and ascension to heaven. So writing of the Gospel of Luke was his way of getting to the bottom of the message and story of Jesus. In his own search to find out what really happened, who Jesus was, he interviewed people to write his book.

Sometimes when I read Luke it feels so dry, because there's so much detail that it's like reading a doctor's report. But if we didn't have Luke and his research, then we wouldn't have the full account of Jesus' birth.

One thing that stands out when reading Luke is how often women are mentioned. Luke highlights women at the temple after Jesus' birth (Luke 2:36-38). Luke also wrote the Book of Acts, and in both of these books, women are mentioned being used in powerful ways.

Only in Luke's account of Jesus' life do we find the parables of the prodigal son, the lost coin, and the lost sheep. This is significant when you keep in mind that it wasn't until Jesus' death, burial, and resurrection that Luke came into relationship with

Christ. He saw himself as the prodigal son, the lost coin, and the lost sheep that was found.

The Gospel of John

John was the youngest of the disciples. Some say he was twelve; others say he was fifteen, but we know he was young. When John was at the final supper leaning on the breast of Jesus, I imagine my son, Bear, leaning on me saying, "The service is so long!" John's perspective was so different, being through the eyes of a child.

John is the only one who calls himself "the disciple whom Jesus loved" (John 20:2). He is the only disciple out of the twelve who didn't die a martyr's death. Most theologians say there were several attempts to take John's life, but his enemies could not execute him. That's why he was sent to die on the island of Patmos where he wrote the book of Revelation. But he was the only disciple who died of old age. Even in Revelation, there is a sadness in his writing. He was stranded on an island but was still keeping the faith. He had been tortured, imprisoned, then abandoned on a remote island. No doubt he questioned himself, "I thought I was the one whom Jesus loved." Blessing doesn't always feel like blessing.

The one whom Jesus loved, the world couldn't take out. But the ones who loved Jesus fell. Peter boasted of his love for Jesus but still denied Him. Everyone else boasted on their love for Jesus, but John boasted on Jesus' love for Him. In our life, we shouldn't be focusing on how much we love God but how much God loves us. John's belief in God's love protected him.

Chapter 6
WHAT AM I READING?

Have you ever read the book of Ezekiel and thought, "I would rather claw my eyes out than read this?" Or is that just me? There are some Old Testament books that are rough reading. If you have ever felt that way, then what I'm about to tell you is going to bring you freedom just like it did for me.

As a young Christian, I was sitting with Uncle John one day and said, "Uncle John, I'm just having a hard time reading my Bible all the way through every single year. I don't know if I can do this. There's some tough stuff in there."

He said, "Well, why are you reading the whole Bible through?"

I said, "Because I'm supposed to."

He surprised me when he asked, "Who told you that?"

"I don't know. It's the Christian thing to do."

But then he said, "You don't have to read your Bible through in a year." What? This was the theologian of the family, the walking concordance, dean of a Christian Bible Institute. I was just as shocked as you are right now.

He made a list for me and said, "This is the list of books in the Bible you should read all the way through—just these books." I felt freedom. He told me, "If you read your Bible through once in your life time, you're good." Do you feel that freedom?

Here is the list of the books you need to read and the order in which to read them:

JOHN	GENESIS
ROMANS	MATTHEW
GALATIANS	EXODUS
1 CORINTHIANS	LUKE
2 CORINTHIANS	1 JOHN
HEBREWS	JAMES
ACTS	1 PETER
EPHESIANS	2 PETER
1 TIMOTHY	2 JOHN
2 TIMOTHY	3 JOHN
PHILLIPIANS	JUDE
COLOSSIANS	PSALM
1 THESSALONIANS	ISAIAH
2 THESSALONIANS	1 SAMUEL
TITUS	2 SAMUEL
PHILEMON	PROVERBS
MARK	

I make sure to read these every single year; then, every year I also read one of the books of the Bible that I struggle with. Once you begin studying the Bible, you may want to dive into the other books. Remember in the introduction, I said that deep calls to deep. When you start digging deep into the Word, your spirit will crave more of it. If you want to get deeper into the Old Testament, you'll see that there are over 400 prophecies told about Jesus in the Old Testament. Jesus fulfilled all of them—not some of them; all of them. Even those difficult books in the Bible point to Jesus. But don't feel the legalism to have to read them. Focus on this list first.

The book of John is the backbone for us as New Testament believers. This is why our list begins with John, which just so happens to be my favorite book of the Bible. More theology comes from the book of John and 1, 2, and 3 John than anything else. For us as Gentile believers, these books, along with Hebrews and Romans, are foundational.

You may be asking what makes us Gentile believers and not Jews. The difference is Jews do not believe Jesus is the Messiah. Their beliefs are centered around the first five books of the Bible, which are called the Torah. There are Messianic Jews who believe in Jesus, but they still obey the laws and rituals of the Torah. As Gentile believers, we believe Jesus is the Messiah, and that He was the sacrifice fulfilling the laws of the Torah and prophecies of the Old Testament. Have you had bacon or eaten a hot dog? I am unashamed to answer yes. That makes us Gentiles. As such, the New Testament is for us.

Keep in mind, a lot of the books of the Bible in our recommended list are written to the Jewish believer. That's okay. Because we also have the books written to and for us. However, if we don't have a foundationally sound belief system as Gentiles and we read the Jewish letters first, we can get messed up.

Notice where Genesis is located in the list. It's toward the bottom. Genesis is obviously important but you can get confused when it comes to stories like Sodom and Gomorah when you don't first understand the book of Hebrews. So Genesis is foundational for us but its not the book from which we build our doctrine.

Let me explain this further. Christians say all the time, "I love the book of James." I'm not hating on James, but here's why that can be dangerous. James 1:1 begins, "James, a bond-servant of God and of the Lord Jesus Christ, To the twelve [Hebrew] tribes [scattered abroad among the Gentiles] in the dispersion: Greetings (rejoice)!"

Imagine you walked into my office, saw a note on my desk that said, "To my wife, Crystal." Then wondering what Bryan said to me, you opened the letter and read, "You're the most beautiful girl I've ever seen. You make the best food. You are everything I could ever want in a wife." When you finished reading the note, would you walk away thinking, "I'm great" or would you think "Crystal's great"? You would think, "Man, Bryan loves Crystal so much." Because it was addressed to me.

When reading your Bible, knowing who the book is written to is key. I can get something out of all scripture. The Bible is God-breathed and God-inspired, but some letters are written to certain people groups.

Now read the first line of James 1:1 again: "James, a bond-servant of God and of the Lord Jesus Christ, To the twelve [Hebrew] tribes [scattered abroad among the Gentiles] in the dispersion: Greetings (rejoice)!" This book is written to the twelve tribes. Jewish believers are broken up into twelves tribes. So as Gentile believers, the book of James is not written to us.

Most of the time when people start believing they must do good works to please God and inherit righteousness, they are usually quoting from James. Jews believe in the law of the Torah. But the law does not believe that Jesus was the perfect sacrifice. The law believes that we have to do something to get something. As Gentile believers, we know that Jesus was the perfect sacrifice and His grace—not our actions—makes us righteous. New Testament books written to the Gentile believer—such as Hebrews, Romans, Acts, the Gospels—talk to us, so we're going to build our foundation from them.

Before you read in your Bible and formulate your whole New

Testament theology around something, read who it is written to before you start basing your belief system on it. You may be claiming Jewish promises when you have been given the Gentile promise which is so much better.

"For by grace you have been saved through faith, and that not of yourselves; it is the gift of God, not of works, lest anyone should boast" (Ephesians 2:9 written to Gentile believers).

Chapter 7
DIGGING INTO SCRIPTURE FOR YOURSELF

Reading study books and Bible commentaries is a great way to learn more about scripture, but I want you to be able to dig into the scriptures yourself. In this chapter, I have listed questions that I ask myself as I'm reading the Bible. These are questions that help me when I am reading to see a scripture or a story in a new way or a different perspective. I encourage you to do the same. At the back of the book, I have listed the questions by themselves, but in this chapter I want to walk you through how I utilize them to help me dig into the text.

Who is the main person in the text?
Pay attention to who the scripture is talking to or about. Does this change the context of what you are reading?

What details do you find odd or different?
Look for objects or places that are named, numbers, or any details that catch your attention. In God, nothing is wasted. When Jesus multiplied the loaves and the fish, He said take up all the leftovers and they filled twelve baskets. Why did they need twelve baskets if everyone was full? Because in the kingdom of God, nothing is wasted. Every detail in your Bible should put you

on a pursuit. It's there for you to find out what it means.

Who are the people that are around in the story?

Zoom out and take a broader view of the story. Look at it as if you were looking from above. Dissect who was in the room or in the area. See the story from other people's perspective. When I look at the story of the man who was lowered through the roof to be healed by Jesus, I'm intrigued by the hearts of the people in the room. I start to ask myself questions: What were they thinking? What was their response? What's going through their mind? Why someone isn't named in the text is just as important as why somebody is named. Let those details speak to you.

Is there any significance about the place?

You'll be amazed at how many locations are mentioned in passing, but with a simple search you'll see all the historical references to that location and how significant the place was in the Bible. You don't have to be a Bible scholar to tie together locations of significance. A simple search on a Bible app with the location will show you what has happened in that same spot throughout Biblical history.

If you read the text backwards, can you find anything that will make you see it differently?

Here is an example of how I do this: If faith comes by hearing and hearing by the Word, then without hearing and without the Word, I have no faith. If one statement is true, then the opposite is true as well.

Sometimes looking at the opposite of what happened will help you see something different. The woman with the issue of blood first said to herself, "If I could just touch the hem of his garment, I would be made well." So the opposite is also true: If she didn't have the right self talk, she wouldn't have gone on the pursuit, she would never have touched the hem of his garment, and she would never have been made whole.

How can this be applied to my own life?

This always is important. What does this mean to me? It's great for the woman with the issue of blood, but what can I do with this? Some questions I might ask as it relates to the woman with the issue of blood. Are there areas of my life where my self-talk needs to change? Do I have the kind of faith that will inspire me to take a step?

Are there any instructions that were peculiar?

Jesus gave many odd instructions to His disciples and to those who received miracles. Start to dissect why.

Continuing with the example of the woman with the issue of blood, touching the hem of His garment seems like an odd instruction. She didn't have any proof that it was going to work. It was faith that made her do it. Even in the Old Testament, you can find instructions to Moses or the people of Israel that are specific. Start to think about why and how it was significant.

Is there something left unsaid and yet it happened?

This happens so often in the Bible. People would do something even without Jesus having to give specific instructions on what to do, and they would receive their miracle. The woman with the issue of blood is a perfect example of this. The Bible says He will give us the desires of our heart, and I've always been curious why he gives us the desires. I believe there's a certain point where our desires become His desires. Look at those instances in scripture and think about your own life where you are waiting for the particulars. Follow the unction of your heart and you'll see God fulfill the instruction.

If you'd like to put this into practice immediately, look at these stories and answer the above questions for each of them:

John 12:1–10   John 5:1–9   John 2:1–9

Conclusion

My hope is that this teaching has helped you see God's Word in new and different ways. Inside your Bible is where you find out who you truly are and what you were created to do. My prayer for you is the below scripture from Ephesians will be made manifest in your life:

"(For I always pray to) the God of our Lord Jesus Christ, the Father of glory, that He may grant you a spirit of wisdom and revelation (of insight into mysteries and secrets) in the [deep and intimate] knowledge of Him, by having the eyes of your heart flooded with light, so that you can know and understand the hope to which He has called you, and how rich His glorious inheritance in the saints (His set-apart ones)" (Ephesians 1:17–18).

There are four things I am believing will happen in your life as you spend time in God's Word. That you will:

1. Know God more intimately through time in the Word.
I believe that as you make a step in reading your Bible, no matter how small, that you will begin to see Jesus in new and different ways. Reading your Bible isn't a religious obligation; it is a relationship with the God of all creation. His one desire is that you might know Him.

2. Find healing.

Healing in our hearts is God's next step in His plan for us. This can't happen apart from knowing Him. Many people have tried to find healing apart from Him to no avail. God's plan is that every dark place of your heart be healed and flooded with His light.

3. Understand the hope to which He has called you.

I heard recently that 80% of Christians don't know their purpose. I find it interesting that 14% of Christians read their Bible. If that is true, that means the people reading their Bible are also understanding their calling. Your purpose for life is found in Jesus and will be found after you get through the pain of your past. God doesn't mind using people who have been hurt and broken along the way, but He also wants to lead you out of your hurt and brokenness.

4. Make a difference.

All of this happens so that you can make a difference in the lives of people around you. What starts with you isn't supposed to stop with you. God's purpose for every single person on this earth is that they would know Him, have their hearts healed, find their calling, and make a difference in the lives around them.

I pray that as you read this and begin to put into action the things we discussed that God will do just that for you!

ABOUT CRYSTAL SPARKS

Crystal Sparks is a writer, speaker, and pastor who is passionate about encouraging people to fulfill the dreams that God has placed in their heart. Raised in the small Texas town of Sulphur Springs, Crystal's life was profoundly transformed when she encountered God in the midst of her difficult teenage years.

In her 16 years of ministry, she has served in the role of Youth Pastor, Associate Pastor, and Lead Pastor. Crystal has spoken for various sports teams, youth events, church conferences, and women's gatherings both nationally and internationally. In 2014, she relocated with her husband Bryan and their two children, Brailey and Bear, to plant a life-giving church. Together, Crystal and Bryan serve as Lead Pastors of One Church.

For additional products, blogs, and studies from Crystal Sparks, visit crystalsparks.org

THANK YOU

Dr. Terry Sparks and Uncle John this book is all from hours of conversations around the dinner table. Thank you for instilling within me a passion for God and His house. For helping me develop a love for my Bible and revealing to me its hidden truths. I don't feel like this book is mine, it is honestly yours. All that is within it you have taught me. Thank you for being my Paul and allowing me to be your Timothy. I love you with my whole heart!

Jessica Shook, thank you for believing in this message and putting it to paper. Your vision of this becoming a book is now a reality. Thank you for giving it heart and soul. You truly are a book midwife! You will never know how much I needed that first meeting at McDonalds. You are a continual reminder that God loves me!

My community group, this book is because of our time together. Thank you for being on this journey of life with me. I love laughing, learning and growing with you! My life's greatest joy is watching you grow!

XOXO

HAPPILY EVEN AFTER

EACH TIME WE ARE HURT IN LIFE WE LOSE A LITTLE PIECE OF OURSELVES.
It is almost as though small pieces are left somewhere in our journey, and each piece forms a path that forms a road which leads to where we are today. From time to time we search to pick all the pieces back up to make us whole again.
We have all been through circumstances that have left us feeling hurt and rejected. In this book Crystal Sparks takes you on a journey to finding your Happily Even After.
It is time for you to start living life on the other side of insecurity!

Find this resource by searching the Amazon store.

GENESIS STUDY

THIS IS FOR EVERYONE THAT HAS STARTED TO READ THROUGH THE BIBLE
And felt overwhelmed. From Genesis to Revelation the Bible tells us the story of redemption. It reminds us of who we are, and teaches us of the God who has pursued us from the beginning of time. Despite all the times we have failed-He has remained Faithful. In the first pages of Genesis, we see the promise of the Redeemer that would come and make everything right. His name is Jesus, and He changes everything. The Bible is the story of our redemption. This is a story unlike any other.

Find this resource by searching the Amazon store.

Made in the USA
Middletown, DE
10 September 2022

72872518R00027